Alvaro

SIZA

Álvaro Siza

teNeues

Editor in chief:
Paco Asensio

Editor and original texts:
Aurora Cuito

Photographs:
Duccio Malagamba

English translation:
William Bain

German translation:
Bettina Beck

French translation:
Michel Ficerai

Italian translation:
Giovanna Carnevali

Art direction:
Mireia Casanovas Soley

Graphic design / Layout:
Emma Termes Parera and Soti Mas-Bagà

Published worldwide by teNeues Publishing Group
(except Spain, Portugal and South-America):

teNeues Verlag GmbH + Co. KG
Am Selder 37, 47906 Kempen, Germany
Tel.: 0049-(0)2152-916-0
Fax: 0049-(0)2152-916-111

teNeues Publishing Company
16 West 22nd Street, New York, N.Y., 10010, USA
Tel.: 001-212-627-9090
Fax: 001-212-627-9511

teNeues Publishing UK Ltd.
Aldwych House, 71/91 Aldwych
London WC2B 4HN, UK
Tel.: 0044-1892-837-171
Fax: 0044-1892-837-272

www.teneues.com

Editorial project:

© 2002 **LOFT** Publications
Domènech 9, 2-2
08012 Barcelona. Spain
Tel.: 0034 93 218 30 99
Fax: 0034 93 237 00 60
e-mail: loft@loftpublications.com
www.loftpublications.com

Printed by:
Gráficas Anman. Sabadell, Barcelona. Spain

May 2002

Die Deutsche Bibliothek – CIP-Einheitsaufnahme
Ein Titeldatensatz für diese Publikation ist bei der Deutschen Bibliothek erhältlich.

ISBN- 3-8238-5580-8

Presenting the work of Álvaro Siza in 80 pages is a daunting and somewhat audacious task, almost rash, and certainly destined to leave out many of his important works. This volume, far from being an extensive review, attempts to show some of the most characteristic features of his architecture through ten recent projects. Paradoxically, Siza's creative philosophy can be condensed to fit on a few scraps of paper: his sketches. If we look attentively at these notes, we will be able to discern all those concepts on which this brilliant Portuguese architect bases his work.

On the one hand, we find the importance he gives to place: one look at the sketches he makes in situ prior to presenting a proposal will suffice. The emplacement becomes the project's nucleus, establishing a dialogue with the site and reinterpreting it, without mimicking it, in order to assign it the role of the foundation of his constructions.

Another of the constants is the profound social conscience. The people who appear in his drawings are not there by chance, but to provide a human scale for his architecture. Siza does not draw up abstract illusions, he constructs buildings for people, constantly bearing in mind the material and spiritual requisites of their users.

Siza's passion for building also shines through in his sketches, where he is able to explore a multiplicity of solutions for the details: anchoring systems, intersections, facings, baseboards, carpentry.... The millimeter-by-millimeter precision allows him to shape the whole and to offer our senses diminutive pleasures.

Sensitivity to the material is another of Siza's facets. Textures and facings are as important in his buildings as is the treatment of light. The lines used in his sketches obey the cutting-up, the assembly, of the materials. The fineness of the stone, the luminosity of the plaster, or the warmth inherent in the wood all blend to bring about comfortable and beautiful environments. Siza's architecture is concentrated in his sketches and plans, simply that, definitively, in the widest sense of the word. Because it is nourished by parameters that are social, historical, formal, technical, constructive and, above all, of an astonishing and imaginative sensitivity that allows him to create tremendously poetic spaces.

This book is a visual journey through the virtues contained in Siza's work, by way of sketches, plans, and some magnificent photography.

Das Werk Álvaro Sizas auf 80 Seiten vorzustellen ist ein gewagtes, wenn nicht verwegenes Unterfangen, bei dem die Gefahr besteht, dass viele seiner wichtigen Werke nicht berücksichtigt werden. Die vorliegende Buch soll in keinster Weise eine ausführliche Übersicht bieten sondern anhand von zehn neueren Projekten einige der charakteristischsten Züge der Architektur Sizas aufzeigen. Auch wenn es paradox anmutet, so wäre es doch möglich, seine kreative Philosophie auf wenigen Papierstücken, nämlich seinen Entwürfen, zusammenzufassen. Wer diese Aufzeichnungen aufmerksam studiert, kann sämtliche Konzepte, auf denen die Arbeit dieses genialen portugiesischen Architekten beruht, einorden.

Da ist einerseits die Bedeutung, die er dem Ort zumisst. Man muss hierbei nur die Skizzen sehen, die er vor Ort anfertigt, bevor er einen Vorschlag unterbreitet. Die Lage wird zum Kern des Projektes. Sie tritt in einen Dialog mit dem Grundstück, interpretiert es neu, ohne seine Identität zu schwächen, und wird zur Grundlage der Konstruktionen Sizas.

Eine weitere Konstante ist das tiefgehende soziale Bewusstsein Sizas. Die Personen auf seinen Bildern sind nicht zufällig anwesend, sondern verleihen seiner Architektur eine menschliche Dimension. Siza ergeht sich bei seinen Entwürfen nicht in abstrakten Delirien. Er konstruiert Gebäude für Menschen und hat dabei immer die materiellen und spirituellen Bedürfnisse der Bewohner vor Augen.

Die Leidenschaft für die Baukunst wird auch durch die Entwürfe greifbar, die es ihm ermöglichen, vielfältige Lösungen für Details zu erforschen: Verankerungen, Überschneidungen, Abschlüsse, Sockel oder Bautischlerarbeiten; über millimetergenaues Design gelangt er zum Gesamten und bietet Sinnesfreuden bis ins Kleinste.

Die Sensibilität für Materie ist eine weitere Facette Sizas: stoffliche Beschaffenheit und Endbearbeitungen sind bei seinen Gebäuden ebenso wichtig wie die Formen oder der Umgang mit Licht. Die Schraffuren in seinen Entwürfe stellen die Verteilung der Werkstoffe dar. Das Edle des Steins, die Leuchtkraft des Gipses oder die Wärme des Holzes vermischen sich zu Räumen mit komfortabler und ästhetischer Atmosphäre. Die Architektur Sizas, die in seinen Entwürfen greifbar wird, ist tatsächlich Baukunst im eigentlichen Sinne des Begriffes, ist sie doch von sozialen, historischen, formalen, technischen und konstruktiven Größen bestimmt, vor allem aber von einer überquellenden und phantasievollen Empfindsamkeit, die ihn ungeheuer poetische Räume erschaffen läßt.

Das vorliegende Buch führt durch Sizas Werk anhand von Skizzen, Zeichnungen und hervorragenden Fotografien.

La présentation de l'œuvre de Álvaro Siza en 80 pages constitue un défi, presque téméraire et condamné à omettre nombre de ses travaux importants. Ce livre, loin de se vouloir exhaustif, prétend souligner certains traits parmi les plus caractéristiques de son architecture à travers dix projets récents. Paradoxalement, la philosophie créative de Siza pourrait être condensée sur quelques feuilles de papier: ses esquisses. En étudiant attentivement ces notes, l'on peut discerner quels sont les concepts qui sous-tendent le travail de cet architecte portugais de génie.

D'un côté, l'importance donnée au lieu: il suffit de voir les croquis réalisés in situ avant de présenter son offre. Le lieu devient le cœur du projet. Il établit un dialogue avec le site et l'interprète à nouveau, sans lui faire perdre son identité, pour qu'il cimente ses constructions.

Sa profonde conscience sociale est une autre constante. Les personnes apparaissant dans ses dessins ne sont pas des présences fortuites mais insufflent une échelle humaine à son architecture. Siza ne projette pas des délires abstraits. Il construit des immeubles destinés à des personnes, gardant toujours à l'esprit les impératifs matériels et spirituels des usagers.

La passion pour la construction se fait également plus évidente dans les esquisses, à travers lesquelles il peut explorer des solutions multiples pour des détails: ancrages, intersections, pignons, plinthes ou charpentes ; le design millimétrique lui permet de créer un ensemble tout en offrant d'infimes plaisirs pour les sens.

La sensibilité pour la matière est une autre facette de Siza : les textures et les finitions sont aussi importantes dans ses bâtiments que les formes ou le travail sur la lumière. Le trait de ses esquisses obéit au découpage entre les différents matériaux. La noblesse de la pierre, la luminosité du plâtre ou la chaleur du bois se mélangent pour donner vie à des atmosphères confortables et belles, comme l'architecture de Siza, concentrée dans ses croquis, et dans l'acception la plus vaste du terme. Car elle se nourrit de paramètres sociaux, historiques, formels, techniques, constructifs et, surtout, d'une sensibilité débordante et imaginative qui lui permet de créer des espaces profondément poétiques.

Ce livre est une visite visuelle des idées forces de l'œuvre de Siza, à travers des croquis, des plans et quelques magnifiques photographies.

Presentare il lavoro di Alvaro Siza in 80 pagine è un compito audace, quasi temerario e destinato a tralasciare molti dei suoi lavori importanti. Questo libro non pretende di gestire l'analisi di un ampio compendio delle opere, quanto piuttosto ha l'obiettivo di evidenziare i tratti più caratteristici della sua architettura attraverso lo studio di dieci progetti recenti. Paradossalmente la filosofia creativa di Siza si potrebbe sintetizzare attraverso solo qualche foglio di carta: i suoi schizzi. Se ci si sofferma ad analizzare questi appunti, si potranno individuare tutti quei concetti sui quali si basa il lavoro di questo geniale architetto portoghese.

Da un lato, l'importanza attribuita al luogo: non c'è niente di più significativo che osservare gli schizzi prodotti "in situ" prima di presentare la proposta. L'ubicazione si converte nel nucleo del progetto, stabilisce un dialogo con il terreno e lo interpreta, senza mimetizzarlo, al fine di rappresentare il fondamento delle sue costruzioni.

Un'altra costante della sua architettura è la profonda coscienza sociale. Gli individui che compaiono nei suoi schizzi non sono presenze casuali, ma conferiscono una dimensione umana alla sua architettura. Siza non progetta deliri astratti ma costruisce edifici per persone, tenendo sempre in considerazione le richieste materiali e spirituali degli utenti.

La sua passione per la costruzione appare evidente sin dagli schizzi, attraverso i quali riesce ad esplorare le infinite soluzioni per i dettagli: ormeggi, interstizioni, rifiniture, zoccoli o carpenterie. Il disegno millimetrico infine gli permette di verificare il complesso e di offrire piccoli piaceri per soddisfare i gusti personali.

La sensibilità è un'altra caratteristica di Siza: le textures e le finiture sono così importanti nei suoi edifici come le forme o il trattamento della luce. Le linee tracciate nei suoi schizzi si riferiscono alla divisione dei materiali. La nobiltà della pietra, la lumosità del gesso o la qualità del legno si amalgamano per definire ambienti confortabili e attraenti. L'architettura di Siza, quella concentrata nei suoi schizzi, è quella che senza dubbio raccoglie i parametri sociali, storici, formali, tecnici, costruttivi e allo stesso tempo quella che si nutre principalmente di una sensibilità straripante e immaginativa che permette di creare spazi incredibilmente poetici.

Questo libro è un percorso visuale della qualità dell'opera di Siza, attraverso schizzi, disegni, planimetrie e di meravigliose fotografie.

Galician Center of Contemporary Art

Santiago de Compostela, Spain
1988–1993

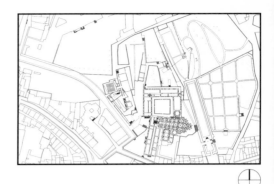

The commission consisted in creating a museum of contemporary art in the environs of the convent of Santo Domingo de Bonalval. The Center is made up of two elements which, coinciding with the entrance, define a small open-air space that contrasts with a platform closed by two of the convent's façades. Access to the garden is defined by the arrangement of these two urban spaces, which face each other, so that this access becomes the focus around which the rest of the buildings are ranged. It is not unlike what happened in the times when the convent itself was built. The layout is in three parts: the vestibule and the offices; the auditorium and the library; and the exhibition rooms.

Der Auftrag bestand darin, in unmittelbarer Nähe des Konvents Santo Domingo de Bonalval ein Museum für zeitgenössische Kunst zu erschaffen. Das Zentrum besteht aus zwei Blöcken mit gemeinsamem Eingang. Sie grenzen einen kleinen Raum unter freiem Himmel ein, der in Kontrast zu einer durch die beiden Fassaden des Konvents abgeschlossenen Plattform steht. Der Zugang zum Garten wird von der Anordnung dieser beiden sich gegenüberliegenden urbanen Räume bestimmt und bildet so das Element, um welches sich wie auch beim Bau des ursprünglichen Konvents die übrigen Gebäude gruppieren. Der Raumplan Konzeption besteht aus drei Blöcken, nämlich der Eingangshalle und den Büroräumen, dem Auditorium und der Bibliothek sowie den Ausstellungsräumen.

La commande portait sur la création d'un musée d'art contemporain aux alentours du couvent de Santo Domingo de Bonalval. Le centre est constitué de deux volumes qui, coïncidant en leur entrée, définissent un petit espace à l'air libre qui offre un contraste avec une plate-forme fermée par les deux façades du couvent. L'accès au jardin est défini par la disposition de ces deux espaces urbains – qui se font face – et se transforme ainsi en élément autour duquel s'articule le reste des bâtiments, comme ce fut déjà le cas lors de la construction du couvent lui-même. L'ensemble se répartit en trois volumes qui accueillent respectivement le hall et les bureaux, l'auditorium et la bibliothèque et enfin les salles d'exposition.

L'incarico consisteva nel progettare un museo di arte contemporanea nelle immediate vicinanze del convento di Santo Domingo de Bonalval. Il centro é formato da due volumi aventi l'entrata in comune, definita da un piccolo spazio all'aria aperta che si contrappone alla piattaforma chiusa tra le due facciate del convento. L'accesso al giardino viene definito dalla disposizione di questi due spazi urbani – collocati uno di fronte all'altro – in modo tale che il giardino stesso si converte nell'elemento attorno al quale si articola il resto dell'edificato; così come accadde anche per la costruzione del medesimo convento. Il programma funzionale si suddivide in tre volumi che ospitano rispettivamente l'entrata e i vari studi, l'auditorio, la biblioteca e le sale espositive

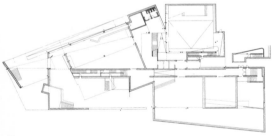

0   5   10

Semi-basement   Halbsouterrain
Étage semi-cellier   Piano semi interrato

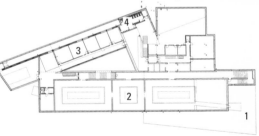

Ground floor   Erdgeschoss
Rez-de-chaussée   Piano terra

1. Access	1. Eingang
2. Exhibition rooms	2. Ausstellungsräume
3. Offices	3. Büroräume
4. Lavatories	4. Toiletten
5. Patio	5. Hof
6. Lanterns	6. Oberlichter
1. Accès	1. Accesso
2. Salles d'exposition	2. Sale espositive
3. Bureaux	3. Uffici
4. Toilettes	4. Toilettes
5. Patio	5. Patio
6. Lucarnes	6. Lucernari

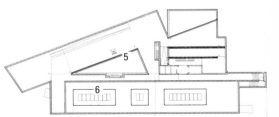

First floor   Erstes Obergeschoss
Premier étage   Piano prime

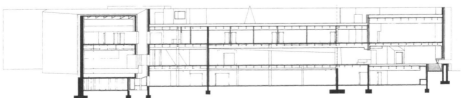

Longitudinal section Längsschnitt
Section longitudinale **Sezione longitudinale**

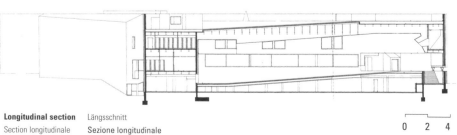

Longitudinal section   Längsschnitt
Section longitudinale   **Sezione longitudinale**

0   2   4

The Vieira de Castro House

Vila Nova de Familaçao, Portugal
1984–1994

The house is on one of the hills that dominate the city of Vila Nova de Familaçao. Because of the sloped terrain, the construction was set on an artificial terrace at the opposite end of the entrance to the property. The house, a two-story affair, is seated on a wooded hillside and opens out to the south with terraces and porches which have magnificent views of the city. The ground floor is of some formal complexity with the dialogue between the walls, the horizontal niches, and the way the natural light enters. The pool operates as a prolongation of the building and of the path between the rocky hillside and the north façade.

Das Haus liegt auf einem der Hügel, die sich über der Stadt Vila Nova de Familaçao erheben. Aufgrund der Abschüssigkeit des Geländes wurde es, dem Zugang zu dem Anwesen gegenüberliegend, auf künstlichen Terrassen errichtet. Das zweigeschossige Wohnhaus lehnt sich an einen baumbewachsenen Hang und öffnet sich gegen Süden hin durch Terrassen und Vorbauten, von denen aus man einen großartigen Ausblick auf die Stadt hat. Das Erdgeschoss zeichnet sich durch formale Komplexität aus. Diese entsteht durch den Dialog zwischen den Wänden, den horizontal verlaufenden Hohlräumen und den mannigfaltigen Öffnungen, die den Einfall von Tageslicht gestatten. Der Swimmingpool fungiert als Verlängerung des Gebäudes und als Verbindungsglied mit dem zwischen dem Felsabhang und dem Eingang an der Nordfassade verlaufenden Weg.

La maison est située sur une des collines qui dominent la ville de Vila Nova de Familaçao. En raison de l'inclinaison du terrain, la construction a été placée sur une terrasse artificielle à l'opposé extrême de l'accès à la propriété. La demeure, comportant deux étages, repose sur coteau boisé et s'ouvre au sud par des terrasses et des porches qui proposent des points de vue magnifiques sur la ville. Le rez-de-chaussée est caractérisé par une complexité formelle née du dialogue entre les murs, les vides horizontaux et les diverses entrées de lumière naturelle. La piscine opère comme une prolongation de la maison et permet d'articuler le sentier, qui parcourt le versant rocheux de la colline, et l'accès de la façade nord.

La casa è ubicata in cima a una delle colline che dominano la città di Vila Nova de Familaçao. A causa della pendenza del terreno l'edificio fu costruito su un terrazzamento articificiale nel lato estremo opposto all'entrata della proprietà. La casa, su due piani, giace su un pendio alberato e si rivolge verso sud con terrazze e portici dai quali si godono meravigliose viste sulla città. Il piano terra si contraddistingue per una complessità fomale creata dal dialogo tra le pareti, i vuoti orizzontali e le diverse entrate di luce naturale. La piscina opera come prolungamento dell'edificio ed è necessaria per articolare il sentiero che passa tra la falda rocciosa della collina e l'entrata nella facciata a nord.

Ground floor   Erdgeschoss
Rez-de-chaussée   **Piano terra**

First floor   Erstes Obergeschoss
Premier étage   **Primo piano**

0   1   2

Elevation   Aufriss

Élévation   **Prospetto**

Longitudinal section   Längsschnitt

Section longitudinale   **Sezione longitudinale**

0 2 4

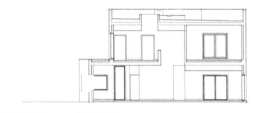

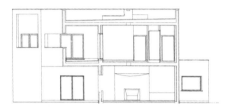

Cross sections   Querschnitte
Sections transversales   **Sezioni trasversali**

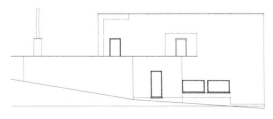

Elevations   Aufrisse
Élévations   **Prospetti**

0 1 2

Faculty of Architecture
University of Oporto

Oporto, Portugal
1986–1996

The Faculty of Architecture of the University of Oporto is on the northwestern angle of a triangular site. The building has two wings that converge on a gardened patio. The lowest side, with a façade that overlooks the Duero River, is divided into five buildings, four of them five-story structures with an identical distribution (classrooms and offices) and a gallery of a single story that connects all of the buildings in the complex by a subterranean tunnel. The other wing houses administration offices, one exhibition room, different size auditoriums, and a library that is one of the truly sublime places in the entire complex. The singular character of the reading room is due to a large skylight in the form of a keel of translucent glass that illuminates the double height room with its bookshelves.

Die Architekturfakultät von Porto liegt an der nordwestlichen Spitze eines dreieckigen Grundstücks und besteht aus zwei Flügeln, die in einem begrünten Hof zusammenlaufen. Die untere Flanke mit einer zum Douro hin gerichteten Fassade ist in fünf Gebäude unterteilt: vier fünfgeschossige mit identischem funktionellem Konzept (Hörsäle und Büroräume) und eine aus nur einem Stockwerk bestehende Galerie, die unterirdisch sämtliche Gebäude der Anlage miteinander verbindet. Der andere Flügel beherbergt die Verwaltungsbüros, einen Ausstellungsraum, unterschiedlich große Auditorien sowie eine Bibliothek. Diese ist einer der erhebendsten Räume der Fakultät. Die Einzigartigkeit des Lesesaals rührt von einem großen, kielförmigen Oberlicht aus lichtdurchlässigem Glas her, das den doppelt raumhohen Saal, um welchen die Bücherregale angeordnet sind, mit Helligkeit versorgt.

La Faculté d'architecture de Porto, qui se situe au sommet nord-est d'un site triangulaire, comporte deux ailes qui convergent en un patio paysager. Le côté inférieur, avec une façade donnant sur le Duero, se divise en cinq corps de bâtiment : quatre de cinq étages avec une configuration similaire (salles de cours et bureaux) et une galerie d'un seul étage qui connecte, sous le niveau du sol, tous les édifices du complexe. L'autre aile accueille les bureaux de l'administration, une salle d'exposition, des auditoriums de tailles différentes et une bibliothèque. Celle-ci est un des espaces sublimes de la faculté. Le caractère singulier de la salle de lecture est suscité par une grande claire-voie en forme de quille de verre translucide, illuminant le double espace autour duquel sont disposées les étagères des livres.

La facoltà di Architettura di Oporto, ubicata al vertice di un lotto triangolare rivolto a nord-ovest, consta di due ali che convergono in un patio con giardino. Il fianco più basso, il cui fronte si affaccia sul Duero, si divide in cinque edifici: quattro piani su cinque hanno lo stesso programma (aule e uffici) e un collegamento sotterraneo che occupa un solo livello unisce tutti gli edifici del complesso. L'altro fianco accoglie uffici amministrativi, una sala espositiva, auditori di diverse dimensioni e una biblioteca, che rappresenta uno degli spazi più sublimi di tutta la facoltà. La natura peculiare della sala di lettura è data dal lucernario a forma di chiglia in cristallo traslucido, che illumina il doppio spazio attorno al quale sono organizzati gli scaffali per i libri.

Ground floor   Erdgeschoss
Rez-de-chaussée   **Piano terra**

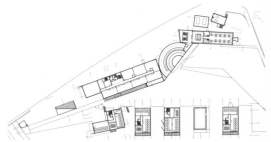

Second floor   Zweites Obergeschoss
Deuxième étage   **Piano secondo**

First floor   Erstes Obergeschoss
Premier étage   **Piano primo**

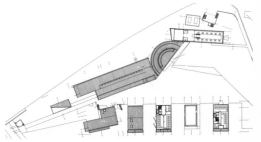

Third floor   Drittes Obergeschoss
Troisième étage   **Piano terzo**

0   10   20

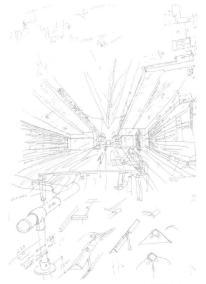

Library sketch   Entwurf für die Bibliothek
Esquisse de la bibliothèque   *Schizzo della biblioteca*

Faculty complex sketch   Entwurf der Gesamtanlage
Esquisse de l'ensemble   *Schizzo d'insieme*

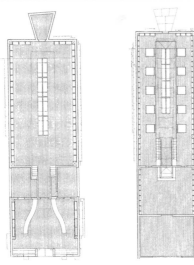

Cross sections of the library
Sections transversales de la bibliothèque

Querschnitte der Bibliothek
Sezioni trasversali della biblioteca

The ground floor and second floor of the library
Rez-de-chaussée et premier étage de la bibliothèque

Erdgeschoss und erstes Obergeschoss der Bibliothek
Piano terra e primo piano della biblioteca

Church of Santa María

Marco de Canavezes, Portugal
1990–1996

The Church of Santa María is only one part of a religious complex which is also planned to include an auditorium, a catechism school, and the priest's living quarters. The project, on a steep incline, occupies two stories, the upper one an assembly room and the lower the funeral chapel. The different style of these two spaces is already patent in the entrances on both sides. The chapel constitutes the foundation of the church itself and generates a stable, fixed level for the building. With its granite walls and its cloister, it establishes a distance from the hubbub of the neighboring street. The main nave is entered by a side door of glass or by a large wooden door, and offers beautiful views of the Valley of Marco de Canavezes.

Die Marienkirche ist nur ein Teil einer kirchlichen Anlage, die darüber hinaus ein Auditorium, eine Katechismus-Schule und die Wohnung des Pfarrers umfasst. Das an einem steilen Abhang gelegene Projekt ist in zwei Ebenen gegliedert. Auf der oberen befindet sich der Versammlungsraum und auf der unteren die Grabeskapelle. Die unterschiedlichen Merkmale dieser beiden Räume werden bereits an deren Eingängen deutlich. Die Grabeskapelle ist der Unterbau der eigentlichen Kirche und bildet eine stabile Ebene, auf der das Gebäude sitzt. Darüber hinaus schafft sie mit ihren Granitmauern und dem Kreuzgang eine Distanz zur nahegelegenen, verkehrsreichen Landstraße. Der Zugang zum Hauptschiff ist sowohl über eine gläserne Seitentür als auch über ein großes Holztor möglich, von dem aus man einen großartigen Ausblick auf das Tal Marco de Canavezes hat.

L'église de Santa María n'est qu'une partie d'un complexe religieux qui inclut, par ailleurs, un auditorium, une école de catéchèse et les foyers de la paroisse. Le projet, situé sur une pente aiguë, se développe sur deux niveaux : l'assemblée est en haut, la chapelle mortuaire en bas. Les différentes caractéristiques de ces deux espaces se révèlent dès les accès des deux étages. La chapelle mortuaire constitue le ciment de l'église elle-même et engendre un niveau stable et fixe pour asseoir l'édifice. Par surcroît, avec ses murs de granit et son cloître, elle établit une distance vis-à-vis de l'effervescence de la route voisine. La nef principale est accessible par une porte latérale vitrée mais aussi par large portail en bois qui offre des points de vue magnifiques sur la vallée de Marco de Canavezes.

La chiesa si Santa Maria rappresenta solo una parte di un più ampio complesso religioso, che prevede inoltre un auditorio, una scuola di catechismo, e l'alloggio del parroco. Il progetto, situato su un terreno in forte declivio, si sviluppa su due livelli: in quello superiore è ubicata l'assemblea mentre in quello inferiore la cappella mortuaria. Le diverse caratteristiche di entrambi gli spazi risultano evidenti sin dagli accessi. La cappella mortuaria costituisce la base della chiesa stessa, creando un livello saldo e stabile su cui si erige l'edificio. Inoltre, grazie alla presenza del chiostro ed ai muri di granito, la chiesa riesce a stabilire un certo distacco con la strada trafficata e rùmorosa ad essa adiacente. L'accesso alla navata principale avviene per mezzo di una porta vetrata laterale e di un gran portone di legno, quest'ultimo si affaccia su un meraviglioso panorama: la Valle de Marco Canavezes.

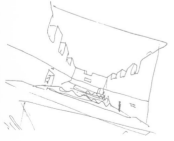

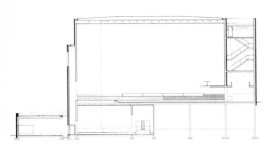

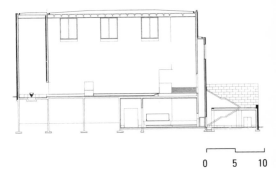

Longitudinal sections Längsschnitte
Sections longitudinales Sezioni longitudinali

0   5   10

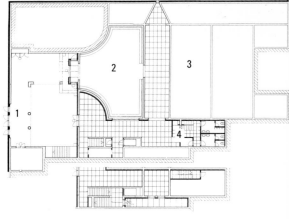

Plan   Grundriss
Étage   Pianta

1. **Entrance**   1. Eingang
2. **Presbytery**   2. Presbyterium
3. **Nave**   3. Schiff
4. **Lavatories**   4. Toiletten

1. Entrée   1. Accesso
2. Presbytère   2. Presbiterio
3. Nef   3. Navata
4. Toilettes   4. Servizi

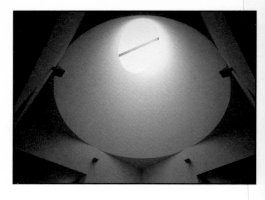

Showroom Revigrés

Agueda, Portugal
1993–1997

The commission for the headquarters of this stoneware firm involved an extension project for the already existing administration building. The façade of the new piece was situated parallel and forward of the original, to which it was connected by a high gallery. Siza's part in the project was to place two bodies that were connected to each other: one of them corresponds to an exhibit hall on columns with a stepped roof crowned by a conical lantern; the other houses the offices in a lineal bay with a slightly curved roof. The structure of the complex uses columns and stressed steel walls partially covered with granite plates. The facings are of stainless steel and the finishings inside are of wood. The floors are mosaic, the walls stucco.

Der Sitz des Industrie-Unternehmens für Verkleidungen aus Steinzeug erteilte Siza diesen Auftrag zur Erweiterung eines bereits vorhandenen Verwaltungsgebäudes. Die Fassade des neuen Baus verläuft parallel zur ursprünglichen und ist dieser vorgelagert. Beide sind über eine erhöhte Galerie miteinander verbunden. Der Beitrag Sizas besteht aus zwei miteinander verbundenen Körpern. Zum einen handelt es sich um einen erhöht auf Säulen ruhenden Ausstellungsraum mit einem gestuften Dach, welches ein kegelförmiges Oberlicht krönt. Der andere Block beherbergt die Büroräume in einem geradlinigen Bau mit leicht gekrümmtem Dach. Die Struktur der Anlage besteht aus teilweise mit Granitplatten verkleideten Säulen und Mauern aus Stahlbeton. Die äußeren Tür- und Fensterrahmen bestehen aus rostfreiem Stahl, die inneren aus Holz. Die Böden sind mit Mosaiken ausgelegt und die Trennwände mit Gips verputzt.

La commande pour le siège social l'entreprise Industria de Revestimiento de Gres portait sur l'agrandissement d'un immeuble administratif déjà existant. La façade de la nouvelle construction est parallèle, mais en avancée, par rapport à l'originale, à laquelle elle est connectée par une galerie surélevée. L'intervention de Siza porte sur deux corps de bâtiment reliés entre eux : l'un correspond à une salle d'exposition élevée sur des piliers, avec une couverte échelonnée couronnée d'un puits de lumière conique ; l'autre accueille les bureaux au sein d'un volume linéaire doté d'une couverture légèrement courbe. La structure du complexe est à base de piliers et de murs de béton armé recouverts, partiellement, de plaques de granit. Les charpentes sont en acier inoxydable, à l'extérieur, et en bois, à l'intérieur. Les sols en mosaïques et les séparations en stuc.

L'incarico per la sede dell'industria di Rivenstimento in Grés consisteva nell'ampliamento di un edificio amministrativo esistente. La facciata del nuovo edificio è stata progettata parallela e avanzata rispetto a quella originale, alla quale si connette per mezzo di un passaggio sopraelevato. L'intervento di Siza consiste in due corpi relazionati tra loro: uno di questi corrisponde a una sala espositiva elevata su pilastri, con una copertura scalanata e coronata da un lucernario conico; l'altro è un volume lineare con copertura leggermente curva che accoglie uffici. La struttura del complesso è costituita da pilastri e muri in cemento armato rivestiti parzialmente con piastre di granito. La carpenteria esterna è in acciaio inossidabile mentre quella interna in legno. I pavimenti sono in mosaico e i tramezzi di stucco.

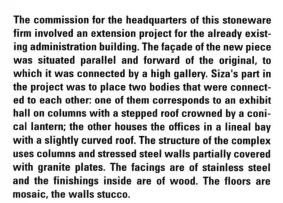

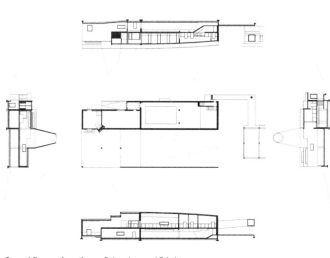

Ground floor and sections   Erdgeschoss und Schnitte
Rez-de-chaussée et sections   **Piano terra e sezioni**

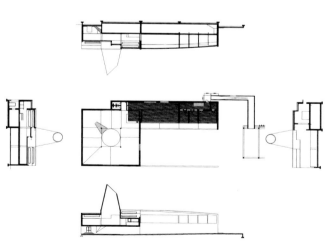

First floor and sections

Premier étage et sections

Erstes Obergeschoss und Schnitte

Primo piano e sezioni

0   5   10

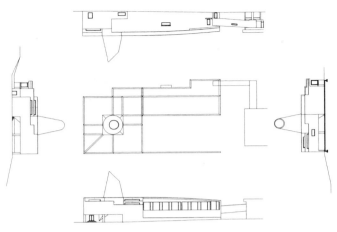

Plan of the roof and elevations   Dachgeschoss und Aufrisse
Toits et élévations   Pianta delle coperture e prospetti

0   5   10

Office buildings on Aleixo Street

Oporto, Portugal
1993–1997

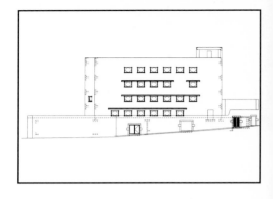

The building, on an U-shaped plan with the open end giving onto the Duero River, occupies the center of the site and is the regulation distance from the surrounding terrain. The ground floor, which will eventually be used for commercial purposes, is still partially buried and occupies almost the entire site. The lighting and ventilation are aided greatly by two patios on the same level. The frame is a stressed steel wall construction built directly on the soil or else on columns, which are also concrete. The closure system, with polystyrene foam insulation, was treated with an ash-colored coating. The interior walls are in white plaster. The floors are varnished wood or, in humid areas, marble. The stairs, elevators, and bathrooms are centralized in a single nucleus in the north part of the building.

Das Gebäude mit U-förmigem, zur Mündung des Douro hin gelegenen Grundriss nimmt die Mitte des Grundstücks ein und bewahrt den vorgeschriebenen Abstand zu den Nachbargrundstücken. Das Erdgeschoss, das bei Gelegenheit für kommerzielle Zwecke genutzt werden soll, liegt teilweise unter der Erde und nimmt nahezu die gesamte Parzelle ein. Zwei Innenhöfe auf derselben Ebene sorgen für Lichteinfall und Belüftung. Der strukturelle Aufbau besteht aus tragenden Wänden aus Stahlbeton, die auf dem Untergrund oder auf ebenfalls aus Stahlbeton bestehenden Pfeilern ruhen. Die mit einer Isolierungsschicht aus Polystyrolschaum versehenen Außenwände sind aschefarben und die inneren Trennwände sind weiß gestrichen. Die Bodenbeläge bestehen aus lackiertem Holz und in den Nassbereichen aus Marmor. Treppen, Aufzüge und Toiletten wurden in einem zentralen Kern im nördlichen Teil des Gebäudes untergebracht.

L'immeuble, doté d'un niveau en U orienté vers l'embouchure de la rivière Duero, occupe le centre du site et maintient une distance réglementaire avec les terrains le jouxtant. Le rez-de-chaussée, qui sera éventuellement destiné à un usage commercial, est partiellement enterré et occupe la parcelle dans sa quasi-totalité. Deux patios, qui ont été situés sur un plan unique, pourvoient à l'illumination et à la ventilation. Le système structurel est à base de murs porteurs en béton armé, reposant sur le terrain ou sur des piliers, également en béton. Les fermetures, avec une isolation en polystyrène expansé, ont été traitées avec une application de couleur cendre et les séparations intérieures avec du stuc blanc. Le sol est couvert de parquet vernis ou de marbre, dans les zones humides. Les installations – escaliers, ascenseurs et toilettes – sont centralisées en un noyau unique dans la partie nord du bâtiment.

L'edificio, con pianta a forma di "U" orientata verso la foce del fiume Duero, occupa il centro dell'area di intervento e rispetta le leggi che regolano le distanze con i terreni limitrofi. Il piano terra che probabilmente verrà destinato ad uso commerciale, è parzialmente interrato e occupa quasi la totalità della parcella. L'illuminazione e la ventilazione si ottengono grazie a due patii posti allo stesso livello. La maglia strutturale è costituita da muri portanti in cemento armato che a loro volta si appoggiano sul terreno o su pilastri, anch'essi in cemento. Gli infissi, con isolamento di poliesterene espanso, sono stati trattati con un rivestimento color cenere, mentre le tramezze interne sono state stuccate di bianco. I pavimenti sono in legno verniciato o trattate con marmo nelle zone umide. Il blocco delle istallazioni – scale, ascensore e servizi – é stato raggruppato in un unico nucleo situato nella parte nord dell'edificio.

Sections   Schnitte

Sections   Sezioni

0   5   10

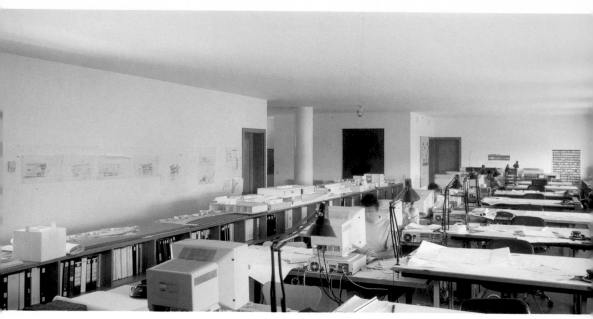

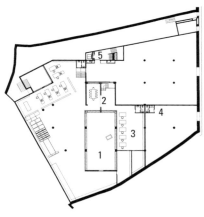

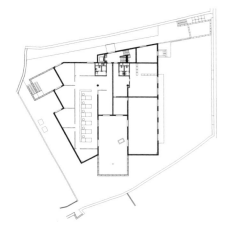

0   5   10

Semi-basement plan   Souterrain
Étage semi-cellier   Piano semi-interrato

Type plan   Geschossgrundriss
Étage type   Piano tipo

1. Patio   1. Hof
2. Conference room   2. Konferenzraum
3. Work room   3. Arbeitsraum
4. Lavatories   4. Toiletten
5. Access   5. Eingang

1. Patio   1. Patio
2. Salle de réunion   2. Sala di riunioni
3. Salle de travail   3. Aula di lavoro
4. Toilettes   4. Servizi
5. Accès   5. Ingresso

The Serralves Foundation

Oporto, Portugal
1991–1999

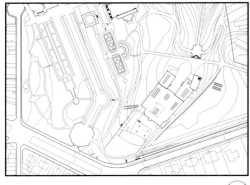

The new Museum of Contemporary Art of Oporto is on the Quinta de Serralves, a 1930s holding that contains different residential cores surrounded by gardens, woods, and fields. The museum is a new autonomous building, independent of the other, earlier ones. It was raised on land that was formerly agrarian. The selection of this site is based on its closeness to the main street of the complex and the absence of large trees, which would have had to be cut down. The building project, which constitutes two volumes connected by a patio, is on a north-south axis. The steep incline of the terrain is not seen in the hip slanted roof because the difference in grade is absorbed on the ground floor. Public access to the building is through the highest level by way of the property's perimeter wall.

Das neue Museum für zeitgenössische Kunst von Porto hat seinen Sitz in der Quinta de Serralves. Dieses Anwesen aus den 30er Jahren besteht aus mehreren von Gartenanlagen, Wäldern und Wiesen umgebenen Wohneinheiten. Das Museum ist ein neues eigenständiges, von den bereits vorhandenen unabhängiges Gebäude und befindet sich dort, wo vormals die Obst- und Gemüsegärten lagen. Das Grundstück wurde wegen seiner Nähe zur Hauptstraße des Geländes gewählt. Außerdem waren keine hohen Bäume vorhanden, die hätten gefällt werden müssen. Das aus zwei durch einen Hof verbundenen Körpern bestehende Projekt wurde entlang einer Nordsüdachse entwickelt. Das geneigte Dach läßt die starke Unebenheit des Geländes nicht vermuten, da die unterschiedlichen Ebenen im Untergeschoss ausgeglichen wurden. Der Zugang für die Öffentlichkeit erfolgt auf der höchsten Ebene durch eine Öffnung in der Umschließungsmauer des Anwesens.

Le nouveau Musée d'art contemporain de Porto a son siège dans la Quinta de Serralves, une propriété des années trente comportant de nombreux noyaux résidentiels, entourés de jardins, de bois et de prairies. Le musée constitue un nouvel édifice autonome et indépendant de l'existant et se situe sur les terrains précédemment occupés par les jardins. Le choix du site est fondé sur la proximité de l'avenue principale du complexe et sur l'absence de grands arbres, qui auraient dû être abattus. Le projet, comportant deux volumes connectés par un patio, se développe selon un axe nord-sud. La forte dénivellation du terrain ne se reflète pas dans l'inclinaison du toit, la différence de niveau étant absorbée par le rez-de-chaussée. L'accès au public est réservé au niveau le plus haut, par une ouverture dans le mur d'enceinte de la propriété.

La sede del nuovo Museo di Arte Contemporanea di Oporto si trova nella Quinta de Serralves, una proprietà degli anni trenta, ed è costituito da vari nuclei residenziali circondati da giardini, boschi e prati. Il museo consta di un nuovo edificio autonomo e indipendente a quelli esistenti, ed è localizzato in un'area anticamente occupata dagli orti. La decisione del luogo derivò dalla vicinanza alla strada principale che connette il complesso e dall'assenza di grandi alberi, che altrimenti sarebbero stati abbattuti. Il progetto, composto da due volumi uniti da un patio, si sviluppò secondo l'asse nord – sud. Le coperture non riflettono il forte dislivello del terreno, in quanto la differenza di quota viene assorbita nel piano terra. L'accesso al pubblico è collocato nella quota più alta, per mezzo di una fenditura del muro perimetrale.

1. **Auditorium**
2. **Parking lot**
3. **Exhibit halls**
4. **Offices and classrooms**
5. **Patio**

1. Auditorium
2. Parkplätze
3. Ausstellungsräume
4. Büros und Hörsäle
5. Hof

1. Auditorium
2. Parc de stationnement
3. Salles d'exposition
4. Bureaux et salles de cours
5. Patio

1. Auditorium
2. Parcheggio
3. Sale espositive
4. Uffici e aule
5. Patio

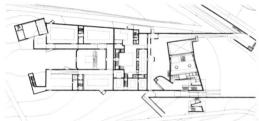

Ground floor   Erdgeschoss
Rez-de-chaussée   **Piano terra**

First floor   Erstes Obergeschoss
Premier étage   **Primo piano**

0 10 20

Longitudinal section   Längsschnitt
Section longitudinale   *Sezione longitudinale*

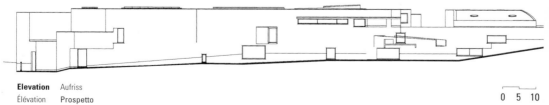

Elevation   Aufriss
Élévation   **Prospetto**

0   5   10

Faculty of Journalism, University of Santiago

Santiago de Compostela, Spain
1991–1999

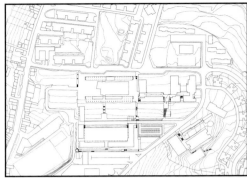

The complex is on the new campus of the Universidad de Santiago de Compostela, the body that commissioned Siza's studio with the project. The faculty itself is a single main volume on three levels: the ground floor and two floors in the western half of its section; and the basement, ground floor and first floor in the other half. A large double-height vestibule creates the interface between these two parts and also includes the entrance and the library. On the north façade, a gallery runs along the whole building and communicates with all of the rooms, making it easy to enter the three bodies that divide the main building perpendicularly. The stairways, elevators, and lavatories are distributed along this gallery.

Die Anlage befindet sich auf dem Gelände des neuen Campus der Universität von Santiago de Compostela, die Sizas Büro mit dem Projekt beauftragte. Das Gebäude besteht aus einem Hauptteil mit drei Ebenen: dem Erdgeschoss und zwei Stockwerken in der westlichen Hälfte; Untergeschoss, Erdgeschoss und erstes Obergeschoss in der anderen Hälfte. Die Verbindung zwischen diesen beiden Teilen bildet eine große doppelt raumhohe Eingangshalle, in der der Eingang und die Bibliothek untergebracht sind. An der Nordfassade verläuft über das gesamte Gebäude eine alle Räume verbindende Galerie, so dass der Zugang zu allen drei Teilen gewährleistet ist, die senkrecht vom Hauptgebäude ausgehen. Treppen, Aufzüge und sanitäre Einrichtungen sind längs dieser Galerie verteilt.

Le complexe a été situé sur les terrains constituant le nouveau campus de l'Université de Saint Jacques de Compostelle, l'organisme à l'origine de la commande du projet au studio de Siza. Ce bâtiment comporte un volume principal réparti sur trois niveaux : un rez-de-chaussée et deux étages pour la moitié ouest de sa section ; un cellier, un rez-de-chaussée et un premier étage pour l'autre moitié. L'articulation de ces deux parties repose sur un vaste hall à double hauteur qui accueille l'entrée et la bibliothèque. Sur la façade nord, une galerie parcourt l'édifice et fait communiquer toutes les salles, facilitant l'accès aux trois corps qui découpent perpendiculairement le bâtiment principal. Les escaliers, ascenseurs et installations sanitaires sont distribuées tout au long de cette galerie.

Il complesso è ubicato nell'area costituente il nuovo campus della Università di Santiago de Compostela, Ente che affidò l'incarico di progettazione a Siza. L'edificio è caratterizzato da un volume principale che consta di tre livelli: piano terra e due piani superiori, situati nella metà ad ovest in sezione; mentre nell'altra metà si trova il piano seminterrato, il piano terra, e il primo piano. L'articolazione degli spazi tra le due parti avviene attraverso un grande atrio a doppia altezza che contiene l'entrata e la biblioteca. Nella facciata a nord un collegamento percorre tutto l'edificio ed unisce tutte le sale, facilitando l'accesso ai tre corpi che sono perpendicolari all'edificio principale. Il corpo scale, gli ascensori e il blocco dei servizi igienici sono distribuiti per tutta la lunghezza del corridoio di distribuzione.

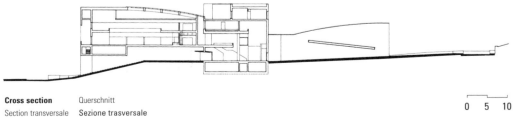

Cross section   Querschnitt
Section transversale   **Sezione trasversale**

0   5   10

Longitudinal section   Längsschnitt

Section longitudinale   Sezione longitudinale

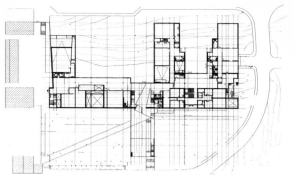

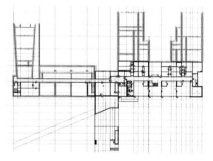

Ground floor Erdgeschoss
Rez-de-chaussée **Piano terra**

First floor Erstes Obergeschoss
Premier étage **Primo piano**

0 10 20

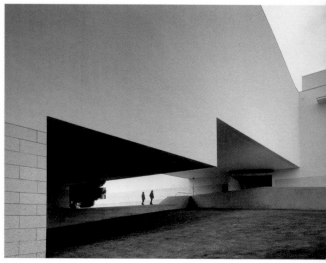

Portugal Pavilion, Expo 1998, Lisboa

Lisbon, Portugal
1995–1998

Portugal's pavilion at the Lisbon Exposition comprised two separate elements separated by a joint construction. The first, on the south, is in fact a large plaza flanked on the north and on the south by two large porticos. These are finished in tiles of different colors. Between them is a concrete slab that describes a catenary curve after the fashion of a gigantic awning. The second body then consists of a building on a regular plan. The three levels are developed around a patio that includes a majestic tree. And at the northern end, the plan opens into a U-shaped patio.

Der portugiesische Pavillon auf dem Ausstellungsgelände in Lissabon besteht aus zwei durch ein bauliches Bindeglied voneinander getrennten Elementen. Das erste, im Süden gelegene ist eigentlich ein großzügiger Platz, der im Norden und Süden von zwei großen, mit verschiedenfarbigen Kacheln verkleideten Portiken flankiert ist. Ihn überspannt eine Betonplatte wie ein riesiges Sonnendach, das eine Kettenlinie beschreibt. Das zweite ist ein Gebäude mit rechteckigem Grundriss. Die drei Ebenen des Bauwerks erheben sich um einen Hof, in dem ein Baum von majestätischer Größe wächst. Am nördlichen Ende öffnet sich der Grundriss und bildet einen zweiten, U-förmigen Hof.

Le Pavillon du Portugal de l'Exposition de Lisbonne comporte deux éléments séparés par une liaison architecturale. Le premier, au sud, est en réalité une vaste place flanquée au nord et au sud par deux grands portiques – recouverts de mosaïques de différentes couleurs – entre lesquels s'étend une couche de béton décrivant une chaînette en forme d'auvent. Le second corps consiste en un édifice à l'assise rectangulaire. Les trois niveaux de la construction se développent autour d'un patio qui abrite un arbre majestueux. À l'extrême nord, le plan s'ouvre pour former un second patio en forme de U.

Il Padiglione del Portogallo per l'Expò di Lisbona consta di due elementi separati da un blocco costruito. Il primo, collocato a sud, è in realtà una grande piazza fiancheggiata sul lato nord e sud da due grandi portici – rivestiti con mattonelle variopinte – in mezzo ai quali si estende una lamina di cemento a forma di curva catenaria come se fosse una gigantesca tenda. Il secondo corpo è formato da un edificio a pianta rettangolare. Tre livelli si sviluppano attorno ad un patio che accoglie un albero maestoso .

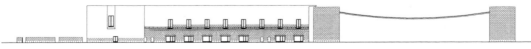

Elevation Aufriss
Élévation **Prospetto**

0   5   10

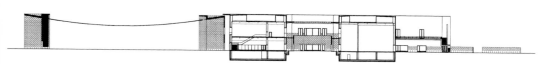

Section   Schnitt

Section   **Sezione**

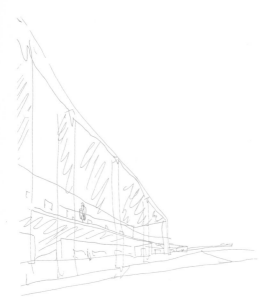

Sketch of the façade   Entwurf der Fassade
Esquisse de la façade   *Schizzo della facciata*

Sketch of one of the entrances   Entwurf eines der Eingänge
Esquisse d'une des entrées   *Schizzo di una delle entrate*

Ground floor Erdgeschoss
Rez-de-chaussée **Piano terra**

First floor Erstes Obergeschoss
Premier étage **Primo piano**

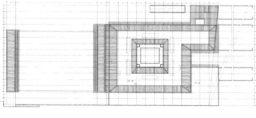

1. Esplanade	1. Esplanade
2. Patios	2. Höfe
3. Stairways	3. Treppen
4. Exhibition rooms	4. Ausstellungsräume
5. Lavatories	5. Toiletten
6. Polyvalent room	6. Mehrzwecksaal

Roof plans   Grundriss der Dächer

Étage supérieur   Coperture

0   4   8

1. Esplanade	1. Spianata
2. Patios	2. Patii
3. Escaliers	3. Blocco scale
4. Salles d'exposition	4. Sale espositive
5. Toilettes	5. Servizi
6. Salle polyvalente	6. Sala polivalente

Portugal Pavilion, Expo 2000, Hannover

In collaboration with Eduardo Souto de Moura
Hannover, Germany
2000

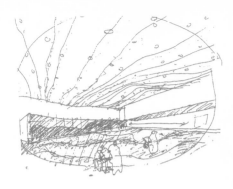

The Portuguese Pavilion at Expo 2000 in Hannover was designed to be dismantled after the event and taken to Portugal. The pavilion's main building, on a square plan, has an arm coming off it that serves as an open-air patio. The duplex distribution of the areas has the exhibit space on the ground floor, with the first floor serving a VIP area as well as an administration room and a small auditorium. The selection of materials was based on the ecological premises of the Expo and on the desire to conflate modernity and tradition. Finishes used include limestone, in the main façade; blue and yellow ceramic tiles, in the patio; and varnished black cork, in the prefabricated iron structure. The corrugated roof of the pavilion is a metallic frame with translucent polyester.

Der portugiesische Pavillon auf dem Ausstellungsgelände von Hannover 2000 war so konzipiert, dass er nach der Ausstellung abgebaut und nach Portugal gebracht werden konnte. Von dem quadratischen Hauptgebäude geht ein Arm aus, der einen Hof unter freiem Himmel bildet. Der Raumplan verteilte die Funktionsbereiche auf zwei Ebenen: das Erdgeschoss beherbergt den Ausstellungsraum, während sich im ersten Obergeschoss ein Bereich zum Empfang von Prominenten, die Verwaltung sowie ein kleines Auditorium befinden. Die Wahl der Materialien wurde vom ökologischen Ansatzpunkt der Ausstellung und dem Streben nach Vereinigung von Moderne und Tradition bestimmt. Zur Verkleidung der Hauptfassade wurden Kalkstein, im Hof blaue und gelbe Keramikfliesen und schwarzlackierter Kork wurde als Beschichtung des Stahlfertigbaus verwendet. Das wellenförmige Dach des Pavillons besteht aus einer mit lichtdurchlässigem Polyester bedeckten Metallstruktur.

Le pavillon portugais de l'Exposition de Hannovre 2000 fut conçu pour être démonté après l'événement et transféré au Portugal. Du bâtiment principal, de forme carrée, jaillit un bras qui dessine un patio à l'air libre. La configuration répartit les activités sur deux niveaux : le rez-de-chaussée héberge l'espace d'exposition, alors que le premier étage abrite une zone pour les personnalités, l'administration et un petit auditorium. Le choix des matériaux repose sur la prémisse écologique de l'exposition et sur le désir de concilier modernité et tradition. La façade principale a été habillée d'une pierre calcaire, le patio de carreaux de céramiques bleue et jaune et la structure préfabriquée en acier revêtue de liège noir vernis. La couverte ondulée du pavillon dispose d'une structure métallique, avec une finition en polyester translucide.

Il padiglione portoghese inaugurato nell'Esposizione di Hannover 2000 venne disegnato per essere, al termine dell'evento, smontato e trasportato in Portogallo. Dall'edificio a pianta quadrata fuoriesce un braccio che disegna un patio all'aria aperta. Il programma funzionale è stato pensato in modo tale che le differenti attività fossero suddivise su due livelli: al piano terra é collocata la sala espositiva, mentre il primo piano accoglie uno spazio dedicato alle rappresentanze, la zona amministrativa e un piccolo auditorio. La scelta dei materiali si basò principalmente sul tema ecologico, tema dell'esposizione e anello di congiunzione tra modernità e tradizione. Venne utilizzata la pietra calcare per rivestire la facciata principale, piastrelle di ceramica azzurre e gialle per il patio, e sughero verniciato di nero per decorare la struttura prefabbricata in acciaio. La copertura ondulata del padiglione è in struttura metallica e le rifiniture sono il poliestere traslucido.

A representação de Portugal na EXPO2000 Hannover realiza-se sob a égide do Ministério da Ciência e da Tecnologia com a colaboração do Ministério dos Negócios Estrangeiros, Ministério das Finanças, Ministério do Equipamento Social, Ministério da Economia, Ministério da Educação, Ministério do Ambiente e do Ordenamento do Território e do Ministério da Cultura.

The participation of Portugal at EXPO 2000 Hannover takes place under the auspices of the Ministry of Science and Technology with the collaboration of the Ministry of Finance, the Ministry of Social Equipment, the Ministry of Economy, the Ministry of Education, the Ministry of the Environment and Country Planning and the Ministry of Culture.

Die portugiesische Repräsentation auf der EXPO2000 Hannover findet unter der Schirmherrschaft des Ministeriums für Wissenschaft und Technik und unter Mitwirkung des Außenministeriums sowie der Ministerien für Finanzen, Soziale Wirtschaft, Bildung, Umwelt und Raumordnung und des Ministeriums statt.

Cross sections   Querschnitte

Sections transversales   *Sezioni trasversali*

0 5 10

Cross sections   Querschnitte

Sections transversales   **Sezioni trasversali**

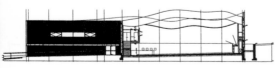

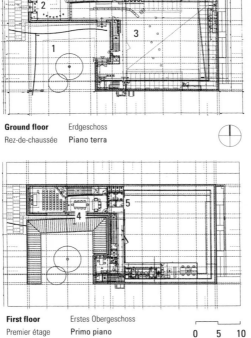

Ground floor   Erdgeschoss
Rez-de-chaussée   **Piano terra**

First floor   Erstes Obergeschoss
Premier étage   **Primo piano**

0   5   10

1. Patio	1. Hof
2. Auditorium	2. Auditorium
3. Exhibit room	3. Ausstellungsraum
4. Conference room	4. Konferenzraum
5. Lavatories	5. Toiletten
1. Patio	1. Patio
2. Auditorium	2. Auditorium
3. Salle d'exposition	3. Sala espositiva
4. Salle de réunion	4. Sala per riunioni
5. Toilettes	5. Servizi